T0121336

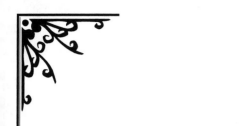

Poetic Reflections

DAVID THOMPSON

ISBN: 978-1-4669-8569-8 (sc)
ISBN: 978-1-4669-8529-2 (e)

Trafford rev. 02/24/2014

 www.trafford.com

North America & international
toll-free: 1 888 232 4444 (USA & Canada)
fax: 812 355 4082

CONTENTS

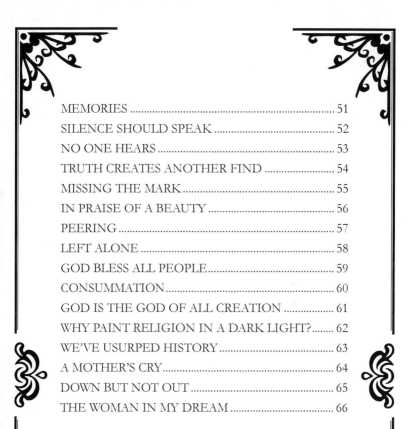

INTRODUCTION

This book of poems is a product of emotions, empathic emotions and perceptions which were experienced over a period of years. The poems may well express thoughts and feelings that others may have.

The poems attempt to address the unanswered mysteries of life. In my case life must go on and life should be one of hope even in the midst of despair. The following pages attempt to include the concept of hope.

CALMING THE WIND

Thousands of years and eons ago
Lightnings flashed, creation flowed
Behind it all there was a glow
That no one knew and few now know
It was God's power making life grow
Until at last there was a show
A thing of beauty which none could show
Until the Christ stopped the wind blow

ECO-SYSTEMS

Eco-Systems are taking over
Making humans just like Rover
Humans are equal to all others
They can't act as did their fathers
The individual has little to say
This runs counter to Eco-Days
Sub servants are we in this system
When in fact we should be pistons
O Ecologists love it so
Making humans less of the show

CAUGHT IN A WEB

I
Our man was caught in a web
He was wrong is what they said
For he was deep in red
And they caught him in his bed

II
The jury thought he was wrong
And ordered he be dethroned
But they misused the Great Tong
Yet his friends were not so strong

III
Now he waits for the last word
He wonders if he will be heard
Or will he be seen like the birds
Wondering why they were stirred?

IV
What will happen to him now?
Will the scene become more foul?
Can he serve the Ship's Bow
With the hate and the howls?

I WANT TO WORK TILL THE DAY I DIE

I want to work till the day I die
Although I hurt and may cry
There's no time for a sigh
I want to work till the day I die

While I love the life I live
I want to give all I can give
The strong desire in my soul
Is to help and make whole

Some may think life is by chance
That there's nothing but romance
But I don't see things that way
I hold out for a better day

There's one thing that I know
I can help to make life glow
Each should do their own part
Give to life with an open heart

THE MEADOW OF
MY DREAMS

In the meadow of my dreams
Tall yellow flowers make a scene
Especially with the grass so green
And my cottage that redeems

There, I've gone for many years
To dry away all those tears
For my wife who was a dear
Here I address all of my fears

So to this space I now go
With the hope none will show
Where I can take life in tow
While I feel the cool winds blow

WHAT ARE YOU LIVING FOR?

What is there to live for if all you do is eat?
What is there to live for if all you do is sleep?
What is there to live for if all you do is peer?
What is there to live for if all you do is hear?
What is there to live for if all you do is feel?
What is there to live for if all you do is smell?
There may be truth that life is a bore.
But surely there's more worth living for.
What then is worth living for?
Love is worth living for.
Freedom is worth living for.
Knowing self is worth living for.
Friendships are worth living for.
Moments with God are worth living for.
What are you living for?

TATTOOED FOR LIFE

Tattooed for life but without clothes
Some heads, small rings but else goes
Birth marks are hidden, all else shows
No place for fig leaves, everyone knows
But is this maturing as the world grows?

THE AWFUL SIGHT

The awful sight of human hurt
Creates pain in inward parts
O the wounds how they must smart
I want to help with all my heart
And I wonder how I can start
Perhaps I can provide some carts
For I must act and change this dark

CAUTION ABOUT DIRECTION

One's desire to take a direction
Should be a done with reflection
Although there be good intention
It could lead to some contention
Acting upon one's emotion
Can diminish one's devotion
While there may be some elation
One could end paying oblation

LIVING THE SLEEP
OF DEATH

The Sleep of Death while still alive
Is like a life that's in a hive
It's captive there and cannot give
Dead to the world but thinks it lives
Yet it's dead to self and in a dive
If only one could break the spell
Of this dead sleep that is a hell
Then one could see and touch and smell
And have real life beyond the shell
And know the call from the true bell

A PARTNER GONE

There was a time when all was well
When the heart would full swell
For I was under a sweet spell
Of a beauty like the Liberty Bell
Now she's gone and life is a hell

NEEDING TO SEE WHAT ALL I'VE GOT

I need to see what all I've got
From this place and from this spot
For I can't move from this damn cot
While lying here and about to rot
Though I be one for freedom fought
Officials want to make life hot
And they forget about our lot
How through blood freedom was bought
Yet to this place I have been brought
While the ungrateful were never sought

THE SOLDIER'S CROSS AND
THE PUBLIC SQUARE

The Soldier's Cross in the Public Square
Should not offend if you're not there
But should offend that some don't care
Nor honor the soldier whose life was shared
For the public people of the Public Square

FROM PRINCIPLED TO UNPRINCIPLED

I
From the hills, to plains and sand
Were a great people in a great Land
But then the cynics began to band
Abusing freedom to take false stands
Counteracting the National Band

II
They divided and did they fan
We became a different brand
Accepting fully just a sham
Now we all have been canned
With false comforts that make bland

O NOBLE ONES,
ARE WE BECOMING?

O Noble Ones, are we becoming?
A people whose letters cannot be written
A people whose Documents have been mittened
A people whose light has a tear
A people whose freedom now seems rare
O Noble Ones, are we becoming?
A people who talk but will not walk
A people of right but then balk
A people for self not sacrifice
A people who let wrong suffice
O Noble Ones, should we not be?
A people holy in Liberty
A people desiring all be free
A people hoping from sea to sea
A people governing and helping be
O Noble Ones, are we becoming?

NO MORE FUN

Now cut that out there's no more fun
Get your knife and get your gun!
Grab your hat to make the run
There is no time for any pun
You cannot hide nor should you shun
Though your life may weight a ton
Now get out there there's no more fun

SOURCE OF SOURCES

Source of sources seems unknown
At first seems active from a throne
Which can't be reached by us alone
But there exist some distant tones
That come and go before we're sown
They are present, then they are gone
But Source of sources makes us at home
Else we will die without light shown

REMOVING THE CORE

Displacing religion, and existence
The Coming of Age is a persistence

I rebel, react and yell out, "no!"
For we will have nowhere to go

The sly are removing the very core
And valued existence will be no more

Is this what Liberty was fought for
Is this the destiny that we bore

We are becoming another product
Being sent through a conduit

FROM MY HEART
TO HERS

From my heart to hers came peace divine
She may not know it but she will be mine
She is such a lady with tastes refined
She is so graceful and a great find
I know I love her, this love will bind

I'M TIRED AND LONELY

I'm tired and lonely and I feel real bad
I just lost my wife, the only friend I had
She made life so good when I was sad
She livened my life and made me glad

Just two weeks ago my Dear said to me
Why not go down to our Tennessee?
The music is grand and moves like a sea
The people are happy as any can see

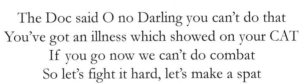

The Doc said O no Darling you can't do that
You've got an illness which showed on your CAT
If you go now we can't do combat
So let's fight it hard, let's make a spat

Two weeks have passed, my Baby's gone
I'm overwhelmed and I'm now alone
I still think that she will come home
But I know better from the silent tones

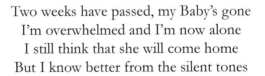

I'm tired and lonely and feel real bad
I just lost my wife, the best friend I had
She made life so good when I was sad
She livened my life and made me glad

IN THE TOMBS OF NOTHING

In the tombs of nothing I'm afraid I will die
I sit on my bed, I mourn and cry
All is lost, my dreams are gone by
I tried, I failed, I don't know why
Nothing worked though I tried and tried
Now I'm alone without sunshine and sky
Those who know me just pass with a sigh

IS IT DREAMS THAT
HELP US SEE?

Is it dreams that help us see
What's out there that cannot be
Beyond the confines of the trees
Or is there space where minds agree
Where travelling time is set free
Free from this world's captivity
Free from the pain to rhapsody

IN THE SHADOWS OF THE NIGHT

In the shadows of the dark night
When there appears little light
Comes the demons who lead fright
And take away all of one's sight
One can resist with God's might

I'VE BEEN REDEEMED

I've been redeemed, I know not why
God gave me life and heavenly sky
So I'll head out and really try
To change that which won't reply
Because my God is very nigh

LIVING WITHOUT
GOD IS AMERICA'S PROBLEM

Living without God is America's problem
It's all about who is Sovereign

Philosophers are nipping at all of us
Misusing God's name as they cuss

But they are dying in their fuss
They want their god or they'll bust

Yet here we are and standing tall
While they're waiting for us to fall

America's the one who heard the call
Freedom and religion makes them gall

Should we listen as they go down
Or continue in our strong sound?

Living without God is America's problem
It's all about who is the Sovereign

A PURPOSE FOR EXISTENCE

Does every tiny little plant
Have a purpose, even an ant?

Instinctualness is not enough
For there should be the right stuff

Coming from God in heaven above
Who thus created out of love

But tension of love and survival
Shows the need for a revival

A purpose for life does exist
Can love win out and fix it?

I'M FEELING BETTER,
I REALLY AM

I'm feeling better, I really am
God came my way, gave me a hand
Now I know that I can stand
God's deliverance removed the brand
I was captured in the world's quick-sand

TAKING LEAVE OF ONE'S SENSES

Taking leave of one's senses
Forgetting about a consensus
Can lead to being a wanderer
Causing one to go too far
Especially if no one cares
To help in personal repairs
Yet there can be a freedom-ness
That can lead one to be the best
But one should not go overboard
Listening to voices one can't afford

MOST FRIENDS AND MENTORS
HAVE PASSED AWAY

Most friends and mentors have passed away
They were good to me and in every way
They encouraged me in what I should say
They supported me above the fray
They even taught me how to pray
They were glad to see me though turning gray
And now I wonder who's next to lay

LEGION AND US

Legions may exist in each of us
Some pronounced, some less a fuss

The self may curb some of the Legions
And even accept some of the lesions

But they still create much confusion
One dare not say they're an illusion

O THE PAIN YOU'VE CAUSED IN ME

O the pain you've caused in me
When you took away my She
She was the one who gave me glee
She was the one who was my Bee
She was the one who made me free
She was the one who could agree
O the pain you've caused in me

DIVIDED

First to the left
Then to the right
First to the peace
Then to the fight
First to the good
Then to the plight
First to the Light
Then to the night
First to the land
Then to the sand
First to the voice
Then to the noise

OUR FLAG FLIES

Off in the distance our Flag flies
Because of nobility and sacrifice
But some treat Her like rolling dice
They do so and don't think twice
Yet our Flag stands with no disguise
While others finger and think it wise

AT A LOSS

I'm at a loss in what I am doing
And cannot help what is brewing

I am in a downward spiral
I continue in this whirl

What comes next I do not know
But this I know I cannot show

If I weren't so damn old
I'd head out and just crow

But as it is I sit and growl
Because I can no longer prowl

THREE WENT IN BUT TWO
CAME OUT

Three came in but two came out
No one knew what it was all about
Some had thought there was a bout
Because there were some awful shouts
But then some learned that one had gout
And one was left and couldn't route

LORD LET ME
GET HOME TONIGHT

Lord, let me get home tonight
Let me have one more fight
Let me walk in Your Light
Let me hold my loved one tight
Lord, let me get home tonight

BURY ME DEEP

Bury me deep in the cold ground.
I hope there'll be no awful sounds,
As there're standing upon the mound.
I did have what few have found,
A real full life no one could bound.

NO WHERE TO GO

Where is there for me to go?
I am feeling down and low.
And I have little to show.
I have moved to and fro.
Now I can't even row.

GROWING OLD BEFORE
OUR TIME

We grow old before our time,
The result of time not defined.
And this puts us in a bind,
Making us seem always behind.
If only one could re-define.

A FREE MOOSE AND ME

A moose is free but I am not
Moose can run when it's hot.
Moose can have what they've got.
Moose can find the right spot.
But as it is I am stopped.

NO WAY

If only there was a way,
Where I could spend peaceful days,
Free of envy and the gray?
There I'd live and I'd stay,
Moving only with light rays.

WORDS WITHOUT SOUL

Words come out but have no soul
Is it because I'm growing old?
Is it because I have been sold?
Is it because I fit no mold?
Is it because I have been bold?
Is it because I have to hold?
Words come out but have no soul.

WHILE

I

While days are clear,
While life is good,
While money's there,
While understood,
While time is fair,
While in the mood,
It's time to share

II

While you have one,
While you have friends,
While you have sun,
While you have wind,
While you can run,
While you can tend,
You must not shun

THE LOVING MORNING HOUR

When early in the morning hour
I lose my way and my power
There is one just like a tower
And provides a love shower
How I love the morning hour

CAN I MOVE ON?

Can I move on with all I've got
The property, the furniture, the whole damn lot?

Time is a wasting I dare not stop
So much to do I fear I'll pop

Yet I do think about attachments
Which keep me from real detachments

I'm accustomed to worldly things
Which interferes with life that sings

But can I trust this inner urge
To get me through with a purge?

I see! I see! I dare not wait
For not to act makes me of late

Then off I go with baggage few
Though not secure, life will be new

A DIFFERENT TIE

Accepting of self is a different tie
Than watching the innocent as they die.

THE LOST REBEL

She had rebelled deep in her soul,

The very day she went and stole.

She went to where she should not go.

And in the end she lay there cold,

Though for a time she felt so bold.

She had hit what she thought gold.

That is why some could not scold.

If only she had let some hold.

MOVING TOWARD PEACE

Let us begin with some compromise

Let us be clear with no surprise

Let us the work with no disguise

Let us agree to have no lies

Let us shake hands without dark skies

OUTSIDE A WET AND BLEAK DAY

Outside is a wet and bleak day

But the inside of me is not gray

Life is filled with bright sun rays

Just how much I cannot say

For I can't measure this full bay

THE NOISE

The noise I hear in this place

Is much too loud and a disgrace

It's no wonder that some deface

And try to leave without a trace

This damn noise is worse than mace

MEMORIES

Down the backroad where we walked
Are some memories that help us talk

There was a shade by the swimming hole
The things we did cannot be told

The fish we caught on the river bank
Made us happy with all our pranks

The songs we sang while some baptized
Were about real truth not disguised

The quicksand bubbling from the ground
Caused us to walk where it was sound

The sycamore trees as they stood tall
Saw contemplation of things and all

O those times on the old backroad
Now help us carry the heavy load

SILENCE SHOULD SPEAK

All the loud mouths gets me down

Some have worth, more are clowns

For few wise words can be found

And hot air blows from all around

Silence should speak and abound

NO ONE HEARS

The music plays, but no one hears.

It is because life's full of tears.

And no one cares to face the snares,

Which has some lyrics filled with spears.

And I do know this is not fair.

TRUTH CREATES
ANOTHER FIND

The probability at any one time

Could bring havoc and confine

Or bring the good and divine

Both cause shivers up the spine

If one lives only in one's mind

But truth creates another find

And helps me not to pine

MISSING THE MARK

I
There is no thought
There is no word
There is no sight
There is no sword

II
There is a silence
That can't be heard
From treasure chests
Which were so dear

III
This is because
We live for now
The past and future
Are missed somehow

IN PRAISE OF A BEAUTY

Woman of beauty, Lady of light

Jewel with grandeur, you are so right

You make one ponder, you give insight

You are a wonder, you are delight

You love life's pleasure, you send new heights

You are a treasure, you change dark nights

PEERING

Every so often an image appears

Partly revealed but leaves when near

All of the image is not clear

A foot, a hand and a quick stir

Although it's there, there is no fear

I rather think I like to peer

LEFT ALONE

What else is new she said to me

She seemed to want all of my tree

So I consented to a degree

But she went further than I agreed

And wanted to have all of my tree

I refused her ways and her spree

Now she's alone and I am free

GOD BLESS ALL PEOPLE

God bless all people who fight hard each day

Who have little hope in what others say

Who are without heat where ever they lay

Who can hardly make it on their small pay

Who struggle for the family come what may

Who need some help with a glad sun ray

God bless all people who fight hard each day

CONSUMMATION

A new reality is coming our way

And different from this kind of day

It may be "No!" that you will say

But there is One who gives a ray

With great hope come what may

His name is Jesus who's never gray

He has a room where you will stay

And a bed where you can lay

So cheer up among life's fray

GOD IS THE GOD OF ALL CREATION

God is the God of creation
And the God of liberation
And the God is of all nature
And the God of all creatures
And the God Who is I AM
And the God beyond time span
And the God who's from above
And the God Who is love
And the God Who is light
And the God Who is might
And the God Who forgives
And the God Who always is
And the God Who grants grace
And the God of all race
And the God Who is truth
And the God Who shines forth
God is the God of creation
And the God of liberation

WHY PAINT RELIGION IN
A DARK LIGHT?

Why paint religion in a dark light?
American religion has given sight

Yes it's true the Church is waning
But it's a fact religion is gaining

Ninety two percent now believe
Which has helped our Nation achieve

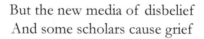

But the new media of disbelief
And some scholars cause grief

They replace God of the heart
And say belief is a human part

It may appear they know it all
But the facts reflect another call

Why place religion in a dark light?
American religion has given sight

WE'VE USURPED HISTORY

We've usurped history tried and proved
With another system abused

Although some truth may come in vogue
Some presenters are just like the rogues

They are zealous to bring to discredit
All acknowledged truth that has credit

It's not new realities that are discovered
But they leave nothing to recover

They do not assimilate but dismiss
Revealed truth causes them distress

They want lock-step and follow the leader
And they won't acknowledge another meter

The Humanists and Secularists are on one level
And consider belief as somehow evil

A MOTHER'S CRY

A car crashed not far from home

Our mother cried, "It is my son.

He's died travelling all alone."

We tried to tell her it was not

But she tried to tell by the groan

Although it was a neighbor's son

Whose mother would soon moan

For death had come and taken life

As the son's head had hit a stone

Then the two cried over death

While hearts ached and sorrow was shown

DOWN BUT NOT OUT

Down but not out thanks be to God

Who lifts us up while I trod

There is always some other day

There is always some other way

When one may feel all is lost

God comes to us as our host

Hamstrung for now one may be

But God has a way to set us free

THE WOMAN IN
MY DREAM

I met this woman in my dream

The nicest person it did so seem

She had red hair with some curls

I knew right then she was a pearl

Her great physique was so just right

I knew that she could hold one tight

She moved with grace and smile

One could see she had great style

Her dress was white in flowery pink

It clung to her as if to wink

Her lovely voice spoke with a "Hi"

And there I stood with just a sigh

O this woman of great beauty

I'd care for her as if my duty